Why this book is nescessary

Frankly, adults have had their own way for too long. If kids want to do anything they have to get permission from an adult. Why? Because adults are in charge. But why are they in charge? Because they are more intelligent? No, most adults haven't got the brain of a grasshopper. The reason is that adults are

    (a) bigger
    (b) have all the money

The trouble is, they own where we live and dictate what we wear, what we eat and where we go. And because they are bigger and have all the money, they think they can pick our friends, decide how we look, what time we go to bed, and even how we breathe ('Don't breathe through your mouth, it's bad for you').

This book tells you how to beat them, so use it and learn to rule your world. Don't let them get you down!

KIDS RULE OK!

Also by Jim Eldridge
The Funniest Joke Book
The Wobbly Jelly Joke Book

HOW TO HANDLE GROWN-UPS

Jim and Duncan Eldridge

Illustrated by
David Mostyn

Beaver Books

A Beaver Book

Published by Arrow Books Limited
17-21 Conway Street, London W1P 6JD

An imprint of the Hutchinson Publishing Group

London Melbourne Sydney Auckland
Johannesburg and agencies throughout
the world

First published 1985
Reprinted 1985 (three times) and 1986

Text © Jim and Duncan Eldridge 1985

Illustrations © the Hutchinson Publishing Group 1985

Set in Linoterm Century Schoolbook
by JH Graphics Limited, Reading, Berks

Printed and bound in Great Britain by
Anchor Brendon Limited, Tiptree, Essex

ISBN 0 09 938150 8

Reasons for not having done the washing up/washed.

There was a spider in the sink and I didn't want to kill it.

I was just about to when the Water Board phoned to say they were turning the water off, and not to use it again until further notice.

My conscience wouldn't allow me to while half the world is suffering from drought.

When I touched the tap I got an electric shock, so I thought it safest to wait.

The water came out a funny colour.

My teacher told me today that soap is made from whales, and as I've decided to become a vegetarian I can't use it.

My skin's allergic to the fluoride in the water.

I don't think it's hygienic to use our water because it's been recycled. My teacher said five people have already drunk our water before it reaches us.

I was afraid to wash up in case I broke something.

Due to the water shortage I thought it was more patriotic to save it.

First the washing-up water was too hot, so I let it cool down. Then it was too cold to get things clean.

We've run out of washing-up liquid.

I've cut my hand and the soap/washing-up liquid might get in the cut.

Reasons for being late for school.

The bus had a puncture and we had to push it into the garage.

Signals from space satellites have been interfering with my digital alarm clock, so it went off an hour late.

I stopped to help an old lady across the road, then I couldn't get back because of the heavy traffic.

I was here much earlier, but no one else was, so I went home again thinking school must have been cancelled.

I got on the wrong bus.

I was doing my biology project and I wanted to see if I could wake up automatically at 7.30. I couldn't.

There was room for only one more on the bus, so although I was first in the queue I let this old lady have my place.

I was just about to leave the house when my pet cat/dog/tortoise/budgerigar fainted, and I had to revive it.

I thought my dentist/doctor's appointment was this morning, but when I got there I found it wasn't.

The kitchen cupboard collapsed on my Gran, and I had to get it off her before I came to school. I might get a 'Blue Peter' Award for saving her life.

The bus driver collapsed at the wheel and we had to wait for another bus.

The bus was hijacked.

They said on the news that all schools were closed because the teachers/caretakers/lollipop ladies were on strike.

8

On my paper round, I spotted a burning building and I phoned the Fire Brigade. Because I was a witness I had to wait and give evidence.

This can also be reworked as:

On my paper round, I saw a car accident and I phoned the ambulance. Because I was a witness I had to wait and give evidence.

or as:

On my paper round, I saw a break-in and I phoned the police. Because I was a witness . . . etc, etc.

I stopped on my way to deliver a message for my mother, and when I came out someone had stolen my bike.

My bike had a puncture and I had to push it to school.

The chain/handlebars/saddle came off my bike.

We were burgled in the night and I had to wait for the police to call to give my statement.

It snowed in our street this morning.

I thought today was a Bank Holiday.

I tripped on the doorstep as I was leaving and sprained my ankle.

When I left home I realized I'd left my homework indoors. I'd left my key indoors, so I had to break in, because I didn't want to come to school without my homework. I went round the house looking for a window that was open, but the only one that was open was upstairs, so I went to the shed to get my dad's ladder, but the shed was locked, so I had to break into the shed. I got the ladder out and put it against the wall and climbed up, but the ladder wasn't long enough, so I started to climb up the ivy . . . All right, I'll sit down, but don't you want to listen to my reason, sir/miss?

Excuses for having broken crockery.

The cat/dog/hamster/budgerigar did it.

It was like that when I came in.

My teacher said you could do that with it and it
wouldn't break because of centrifugal force. It's
my teacher's fault and I'll tell him/her he/she
owes you a new cup/plate/saucer.

As I looked at it, it jumped off the shelf. I think I
must have supernatural powers.

I thought it was made of unbreakable plastic.

I was trying out a science experiment I saw on 'Blue Peter'.

I don't know how it happened. I heard this crash, and there it was.

I was making you a cup of tea when it happened.

I was practising plate spinning to get into the *Guinness Book of Records*. I wanted you to be proud of me.

You said you never liked that vase/jug/cup/ plate.

There must be something in the water that weakens it, because as I put it in the washing-up it just fell apart.

It was obviously faulty when it was made. In fact, I remember it had 'second' written on the bottom.

Earthenware/stoneware always breaks after six months. It's to do with the chemical nature of the soil from which it's made.

How to get more Pocket Money.

Everyone else gets twice as much pocket money as me. I always tell them that you can't afford to give me more because we're a very poor family.

To Mum:
I want to buy Dad a present.

To Dad:
I want to buy Mum a present.

This only works if your Mum and Dad like each other. If they don't use this variation:

I want to buy *you* a special present.

I need more pocket money so I can practise how to handle my finances for when I'm older.

My pocket money hasn't kept up with inflation. (In this case 'inflation' doesn't mean blowing up a balloon. If your suspicious parents test you by asking what inflation means, look scornful and say 'I thought you'd know already.')

I need more money because I'm saving for a set of encyclopaedias.

I need extra money because I've decided to put some money each week in to a Building Society so that when you are old I can look after you.

I've decided to give some money each week to charity. (Use whatever your parents' favourite charity is.)

The bus fares have gone up.

Look and Learn has gone up.

I've decided to give up sweets and things that are bad for my teeth, so I'm only going to buy things from the health food shop. Unfortunately they cost twice as much money, but if you'd prefer my teeth to decay, I'll understand.

My dentist says I've got to eat fruit. The trouble is the only fruit I like is kiwi fruit and they're very expensive.

My friends say you're mean, but I say you're not. Can I have more pocket money?

How to get your PARENTS to buy you something.

Can you buy me this (whatever)? I'd buy it myself but I'm saving my own money to buy you a Christmas present.

My teacher says it's vital for my education.

Do you want me to be the happiest person in the world, or do you want me to look unhappy and make your life miserable?

If you buy me this bike/guitar/piano/computer, I'll be able to earn thousands with it, and then I'll be financially independent.

Everyone else has got one.

Were you a deprived child?

It would be better if you buy it for me now as an early birthday present, because if you wait till my birthday the price will go up.

Can I have these/this new shoes/trousers/ haircut. My friends say the reason I walk around looking like this is because you're mean, but I say you're just poor.

It's an investment.

Reasons for not eating certain foods.

My conscience won't let me eat it while half the world is starving.

A doctor on TV said that sort of food is bad for you.

I feel sick.

They use deadly pesticides to spray these vegetables.

It's too salty, and too much salt is bad for you.

It's too sweet, and too much sugar is bad for you.

I hear there was a leak in a nuclear power station near where these vegetables are grown/ animals graze.

I'm on a diet.

I've become a vegetarian/vegan/Buddhist/ Muslim/Jew/Hindu.

Our school welfare officer says too much food is bad for you.

Your cooking is really scrummy but I'd feel guilty if I gluttonized myself on it.

I've got a loose filling so I've got to avoid hard food.

A boy in our class who ate this is in hospital with food poisoning.

I'm allergic to carrots/cabbage/semolina, etc.

I saw something move in the salad.

This meat pie was once a sweet little lamb/cute baby piglet/happy fluffy chicken.

I don't eat fish – think of all the nuclear and chemical waste and oil spillages in the sea.

I had a pet rabbit/duck once. It was my best friend.

Potatoes/meat/everything gives you heart disease.

Eggs are baby chickens. I'd feel like a cannibal.

How to get MORE FOOD.

You don't want me to suffer from *anorexia nervosa,* do you?

I'm a growing child and my body needs more nourishment.

With so many people dying of starvation in the world, it would be a crime to waste food, so I've got to eat as much as I can.

Food gives you body fat, and with our cold winters I need more if I'm to keep healthy.

Your cooking is the best in the universe, it cries out to be eaten.

You're looking a little overweight, so perhaps I'd better eat that for you.

Someone else ate my first helping while I wasn't looking.

It'll go bad if we don't eat it all now.

It loses its flavour if it's left more than a day.

The chart in this health magazine said I should be much heavier for my height.

I couldn't taste that first lot of pie because I put too much salt on it.

I should eat 2000 calories a day, and I'm 400 short.

The more food I eat the more energy I'll have to help around the house.

At my friend's house they have bigger helpings than this.

The NSPCC came to school today to check if anyone was suffering from malnutrition.

Reasons for not handing in homework.

I left it on the table and the dog/cat/hamster chewed it up.

I didn't realize you'd given us any.

I did do it but Mum accidentally put it on the fire thinking it was waste paper.

We were burgled in the night and it was stolen.

My Dad thought my essay was so good he sent it to the *Guardian*. As soon as they return it I'll bring it in.

The cat was sick on it. I cleaned it up but it smelt so much my Mum wouldn't let me bring it in.

I handed it in and left it on your desk. Have you lost it?

I left it on the bus.

I thought we didn't have to hand it in until tomorrow.

My pen ran out.

I hurt my hand last night going home from school.

My brother filled my pen with vanishing ink for a joke, and when I got up this morning all my writing had vanished.

We had a power cut last night.

Reasons for WATCHING TV.

If everyone stopped watching TV, all the people who make the programmes would be out of work. I don't like watching TV all the time, but you wouldn't want me to be responsible for people losing their jobs, would you?

It's educational.

It's exercise for my eyes.

I'm watching this film because there's an educational nature programme on after it (in an hour and a half).

My friend's cousin's brother knows the man who writes this programme, and he asked me to tell him what I thought of it.

It's only got another five minutes to go before it ends.

I thought the picture went funny, so I'm watching it to see if it happens again.

They're advertising a £5000 prize if you can answer just one question, so I'm waiting for it to come on.

There's an actor/actress in this programme who looks just like you.

Dad/Mum said we're going to have to get rid of the telly, so I'm watching it while I've got the chance.

I'm doing a sponsored TV watch for charity.

This programme is the last in the series. I *can't* miss it!

REASONS FOR NOT DOING SHOPPING

I can't reach the top shelves.

The manager suspects all young people of shoplifting, so they won't let me in without an adult.

I can't read your writing on this shopping list.

Is this one potato or one pound of potatoes?

Granny always pays me for going shopping.

Last time I went you didn't give me enough money.

The shopping bag cuts my fingers.

It's half-day closing today.

The supermarket's closed for redesigning/staff training.

Does 60p taken from a pound leave 20p change?

When you say 'big tin of tomatoes' do you mean very big, large, big medium, medium or small?

I've hurt my leg/arm/ankle.

That was the shop where there was an armed robbery last week.

That shopkeeper cheats young people out of their change.

Of course I'll go shopping for you but don't blame me if I get the wrong brand.

Reasons clothes are torn/soaked/damaged.

I saved someone from drowning. I might get a 'Blue Peter' Award.

I got caught in a hurricane.

I used my coat to put out a dangerous fire.

An old lady was about to be run over. I rushed forward and threw her out of the way, but I got run over myself.

I got mugged.

I got caught in the rain.

I was walking past a fire engine when its hoses burst and water went all over me.

This machine for painting white lines on roads blew up outside our school.

I was savaged by a dog/cat/werewolf.

I was standing under this drainpipe when it collapsed.

It was foggy and I fell down a hole in the road.

I was waiting at a bus stop and this car went through a puddle and splashed me.

A chemistry experiment at school went wrong.

Someone spilled ink on my jacket, and so as not to upset you I tried to clean it off myself. My friend told me acid would remove it.

What jacket?

It was either a seagull or a pigeon that did it.

How to get out of doing household chores.

I'm allergic to dust.

My elbow/leg/arm/wrist/neck hurts.

My bed *is* made.

The doctor said I've got to rest.

I've got/I'm recovering from flu.

The broom falls apart whenever I use it.

I didn't know this was your new blouse, I thought it was a duster.

How do you work the vacuum cleaner without it breaking?

The neighbours asked me if I knew the phone number of the NSPCC.

Why do we need to clean the windows? They only get dirty again.

It's not *my* dust on the floor, why should I have to sweep it up?

Does your nylon blouse go on 'boil' wash?

I don't mind doing the cooking, but last week my friend cut his/her finger off with a kitchen knife.

I did feed the goldfish. I fed it to the cat.

I've done the stew for dinner. I used that tin of meat with a picture of a cat on it.

Reasons for not having bought a Birthday card/present.

I didn't think you'd like to be reminded that you're getting older.

I don't have enough pocket money to buy you a present.

Instead of buying you a present I sent the money to your favourite charity. I thought you'd prefer that.

They didn't have a card good enough for you.

You always say it's the thought that counts.

I've sent away for your present to a mail-order company. I told them when your birthday was, but it hasn't arrived yet.

I sent it to you a week ago. I hope it hasn't got lost in the post.

I bought you a (whatever), but then I found out that Mum/Dad had bought you one as well.

As I was wrapping it up, it broke.

Mum/Dad wouldn't let me give it to you because he/she said you were allergic to it.

I didn't know your size.

I've been saving up for this special thing for you, but when I'd got all the money together the shop had sold out.

The present got stolen.

As I was writing the card my pen broke and ruined it, so I had to throw it away.

I thought your birthday was next week.

I thought you said you didn't want me to get you anything.

reasons for not going to skool.

I feel ill.

The teachers/caretakers/dinner ladies are on strike today.

The school's shut for the elections.

I haven't got my PE/games equipment.

As it's a public holiday today, the schools are closed.

There's an epidemic of measles/chicken-pox/plague at school.

There's a bully at school who says he's going to get me.

They're decorating the school and they've found asbestos in the walls.

My teacher says I needn't come in today if I haven't done my homework.

Three children in our class have got head lice.

Our teacher's ill and they aren't getting a replacement till tomorrow.

Someone said the torrential rain last night has closed the school.

The fifth year are having exams so we don't need to go in.

Reasons for not giving up your seat on a bus.

I'm saving it for my Mum.

I've hurt my leg.

I'm actually an elderly dwarf.

There's chewing gum on this seat and I'm stuck to it.

Reasons For Staying up late.

I need to stay up late so that I won't wake up early and disturb you.

I'm staying up late to see if I can get into the *Guinness Book of Records* for going without sleep for longer than anybody.

I'm getting older now so I don't need so much sleep.

I've got used to staying up late.

All my friends go to bed later than me.

There's a programme on later tonight that our teacher wants us to watch.

I thought you liked my company.

It's lonely/cold upstairs in my room.

I'll go up as soon as this programme finishes.

I've got to tidy up my room first.

The cat's just been sick on my bed.

I don't feel tired.

My head hurts when I lie down.

There's a spider/moth/ghost in my room.

I can't sleep because of the noise from the neighbours next door.

I think there are bedbugs/fleas from the cat/dog/ hedgehog in my mattress.

I'm waiting for my electric blanket to heat up.

Will you read me a story?

You and I never get a chance to talk.

It's bad to sleep on a full stomach, and I've just eaten a sandwich.

I can't sleep when I'm hungry.

I had an electric shock last night when I turned my light on.

REASONS FOR HAVING a PET.

A dog will guard the house against burglars.

A cat will keep mice away.

A pet will teach me to be kind to animals.

They're killing stray cats/dogs at the animal home.

A canary will tell us if there's a gas leak.

All my friends have got pets.

I want an Alsation so that I can win Cruft's Dog Show, become rich and famous and then help you financially.

If you have an animal you get on 'Blue Peter'.

A tortoise is no trouble and doesn't have to be taken for long walks.

I promise I'll look after it.

If we have a dog, next door's cat will stop coming into our garden.

And if you still don't like the fish/rabbit, we can always eat it.

If I had a parrot I could teach it to talk and hire it out for films.

Taking a dog for walks would be good exercise for me.

A dog would fetch your papers for you.

A pet would be a friend for me.

A cockerel will wake me up in the morning and make sure I get up for school.

Reasons for Breaking/ Damaging/ Tearing Household Objects.

I know who did it but I'd rather not say because I don't want to get Dad/Mum in trouble.

I thought you said you were going to throw it away, anyway.

It was working when I finished with it.

The Salvation Army came round collecting jumble so I gave it to them because I thought you didn't want it any more.

I thought it was the *old* one.

You said you wanted me to be a record breaker.

The cat/dog/hamster/tortoise did it.

I've never seen it before in my life.

But you said your new stereo/washing machine was so simple even a child could use it.

The television just blew up when I was nowhere near it.

The springs on that sofa were already like that.. It's probably because you're overweight.

But you've always told me you have to turn the gas on for a bit before you light the oven.

When this bloke on the telly balanced a chair on his head it worked.

When that man on the telly did the same thing you laughed and said how funny it was.

They don't make furniture like they used to.

It just fell off the shelf. They must be doing some building work next door.

Oh, *that* chair.

How to get an Adult to take you to a fair/cinema/ for a meal.

But, Mum, you said you were fed up with cooking.

This film is very educational.

Your favourite actor/actress is in this film.

This fair is just like the ones when you were small.

All my friends' parents have taken them.

After all, you did say you wanted me out of the house.

How to ~~avoid~~ avoid going somewhere.

(e.g. visiting relatives)

I wouldn't want to be a nuisance to them.

It's such a long way and you know I get car sick.

You'd have a much better time without me there.

When Granny kisses me her moustache brings me out in spots.

You always say you wish you had more time on your own with your Dad/Mum/Sister, etc.

I'm ill and I don't want Gran/Uncle/Aunt to catch it.

HOW TO AVOID GOING TO THE DENTIST.

That dentist took out the wrong tooth of a friend of mine.

Did you know our dentist's an alcoholic?

Did you read about that boy who died when he was given an anaesthetic?

Our dentist cuts himself shaving. Would you allow someone as shaky as that with a drill in your mouth?

I'm allergic to anaesthetic.

I had my teeth checked by the school dentist last week.

I don't want to be a nuisance to the dentist, he's so busy.

How to get your parents to move house.

You always say the air/climate here is bad for us.

I don't have any friends here.

The price of property is much cheaper in (wherever you want to go).

The schools are much better at (ditto).

(Ditto) is so near Gran/Uncle/the sea/work.

This house is too small for all of us.

Did you know they're going to build a motorway through here?

If we had a bigger house you wouldn't see so much of me.

They reckon property at (your favourite place) will go up by 100% next year.

Have you heard who's moving in next door?

I'd hate to grow old in this house.

The weather at (your favourite place) is wonderful. You'll feel so much better.

The crime rate in this area is increasing. At (your favourite place) they don't have any crime at all.

They're going to make next door into an all-night disco club.

REASONS WHY VIDEO/ ARCADE GAMES ARE GOOD FOR YOU.

They improve your reflexes.

You can become famous and rich at them.

They're good practice for later on when I learn to drive/become an airline pilot.

You learn how to handle modern computer technology, which is vitally important for getting a job.

how to get your PARENTS to take YOU ABROAD ON HOLIDAY.

The price of food and the cost of living is so much cheaper over there.

Air flights abroad are cheaper than travelling in this country by rail or road.

We're guaranteed good weather.

I'm learning to speak that language at school.

We're doing a geography project on that country.

All my friends have been there.

Are we *that* poor that we can't afford it?

A holiday like that will do you good.

Everyone else in my school/the street/the town/
your work/this country has been there.

How to Avoid Having a Haircut.

It keeps me warm. I'll catch cold if it's cut.

The hairdresser/barber suffers from this disease that causes his hands to shake. Last week he cut off a boy's ear.

Everyone else wears their hair like this. You wouldn't want me to look out of place, would you?

My scalp's allergic to the conditioner they use.

The stuff they put on your hair makes it fall out.

Last time they did my hair, they burnt it.

REASONS FOR GOING OUT LATE TO A PARTY OR DISCO.

I said I would be there and you wouldn't want me to let all my friends down, would you?

There's a prize at the disco to see who's the best dancer, and I'm sure I'll win.

I thought I'd go so that you could have some peace and quiet this evening.

My friends say you never allow me out in the evenings, and you wouldn't want them to think that's true.

Your best friend's son/daughter is throwing the party. You wouldn't want them to think I'm being rude by not going, would you?

It's a school disco. My teacher said he/she wanted to meet me there to talk about my school project.

You get a free meal at this party. I thought it would save you the bother of having to cook me something.

There's a raffle at the party and I've already bought some tickets for it. You wouldn't want me to waste my money and miss the chance of winning a prize, would you?

How to get your parents to give you a clothing allowance.

It will teach me to manage my own finances for when I get older.

It will force me to take more care of my clothes.

I'll buy things in fashion instead of you buying me things that everyone laughs at.

I'll start looking around for the cheapest clothes and therefore save money.

You won't have to come shopping with me, so you'll save lots of time.

I'm old enough to handle my own money now.

All my friends have a clothing allowance.

Do you want me to grow up psychologically disturbed because you won't give me the personal freedom of a clothing allowance?

It will save you the strain of worrying what to buy me.

Don't you trust me?

How to get more money for your clothing allowance.

I'm growing so fast that I need to buy clothes more frequently.

Prices have gone up since my clothing allowance began.

How to con money out of adults.

I'm collecting for poor children.

I owe this big bully money and he's threatened to beat me up.

I am saving up to take you out for a slap-up meal.

All that heavy change in your pocket ruins the shape of your clothes. I'll take it off you.

I'm saving up for an adventure holiday so that you can have some time on your own.

I'm doing a sponsored walk/run/silence/swim/collection.

I read in a magazine that dirty, old bank-notes carry germs.

HOW TO GET A PARENT TO STOP ON A LONG CAR JOURNEY.

You don't want me to be sick on the new sheepskin seat covers, do you?

I feel a bit funny. I think it's because I'm hungry.

I'm dying to go to the toilet.

Did you remember to put the petrol cap back on?

I think we've got a petrol leak/slow puncture.

There was a number plate lying on the road back there. It didn't belong to us, did it?

I think I can hear a funny noise coming from the engine.

Putting it into PRACTICE

In the previous pages, we have outlined practical ways to handle adults. 'Ah!' you scoff, 'that's all right in theory, but what about in practice. Do they work? How do you get away with it? What happens when you come up against really tough grown-ups; grown-ups who are sneaky, devious, and up to all manner of dodges themselves?'

Believe us, our dodges work, and to prove it we are printing extracts from the diary of an arch-dodger friend of ours (who, for obvious reasons, we can only refer to as 'X').

POWER TO kids!

Kids RULE OK!

OR?

HOW TO HANDLE GROWN-UPS

IS PROUD TO PRESENT:

THE DIARY OF X

Sunday 3rd

Auntie Ann came to stay for the day and while she was here insisted on cooking us all a meal. However, as I know how terrible her cooking is, I told her I was on a diet because I was unbelievably overweight. When it came to time for her hideous meal, I told everyone I was just going out for a jog and nipped down to the fish and chip shop.

Monday 4th

Got up. Household in uproar and panic as a result of my secretly putting all the clocks in the house one hour forward last night. Because everyone was rushing around in panic, convinced they were late, I was able to have the best slices of toast and eat two helpings of breakfast without anyone noticing. Took opportunity to ask everyone individually for money for bus fare to school. Everyone paid up, too confused to check with each other.

Tuesday 5th

Bus queue enormous, so I developed pronounced limp as I approached. Considered falling into pitiful heap on pavement to emphasize disability, but thought this might be overdoing it; didn't want to end up being taken to hospital in an ambulance. As it was, sympathetic adults in queue insisted I rest at front to make sure of getting seat on bus. Old lady even gave me her suitcase to sit on while I was waiting – and a couple of toffees!

Wednesday 6th
Problems at school. My lack of science homework has finally come home to roost, purely because my class teacher, Perky Parrott, has started talking to the science teacher, Big-Ears Blunt. (Background note: due to a row over Big-Ears accidentally drinking out of Perky's cup one break-time last term, the two haven't been on speaking terms. I've been able to put this to good use by blaming my lack of science homework on Perky (e.g. 'Mr Parrott took it and said he'd give it to you'; 'Mr Parrott said I was excused all other homework to concentrate on the extra work he's set me', etc. etc.)

Yesterday, drat it, they patched up their row, because Big-Ear's old banger had a puncture and Perky helped him change the wheel. (Perky didn't want to, but he's head of religion and the only one with a jack, so he didn't have much choice.)

The outcome is that I've got to report to the head tomorrow for punishment. Punishment without even a trial! Curses. Wonder what the phone number is of Court of Human Justice at Strasbourg?

Thursday 7th

Do I go to school and take my punishment like a man, or do I stay at home?

Decided to stay at home, it'll give me time to work out escape plan. Went for simplest of all excuses: illness. Used flour to pale face, water to redden eyes, two hot water bottles up jumper to give me a temperature, refused breakfast, and was noisily sick twice. This, added to rumour planted last night of boy in my class with typhoid, led to Mum ordering me to stay in bed. I protested (don't want to arouse suspicion, and it makes grown-ups feel good to score one over you), but she overruled me. Made recovery at 3 p.m. – too late to go to school, but early enough to be able to watch TV this evening ('to take my mind off illness').

Friday 8th
Day of Reckoning

Thanks to yesterday's illness, I had time to prepare my case. Decided 'honest' approach was the answer, grown-ups are helpless against it.

Called in at Twitcher's office (the head), and had fit of nervousness. Admitted guilt, but begged him not to let Perky or Big-Ears beat me. He was shocked at the very idea that I might be beaten, but I hinted that such things went on in their classrooms behind closed doors. (A blatant lie – neither Perky nor Big-Ears could punch their way through a sponge cake, but adults always believe 'there's no smoke without fire' and if they're that stupid, they may as well be encouraged.

On to stage two of the 'honest approach': the shame of being unable to understand the science lessons; Big-Ears' violent temper which terrifies me so much I'm unable to ask for further explanations from him; the awful headaches at the thought of admitting my lack of knowledge; the sleepless nights; the feelings of near-suicide; the relief that it's all 'now out in the open', etc. etc. All the usual garbage.

Twitcher near to tears. Me exonerated. Twitcher to have severe word with Big-Ears. Me excused science homework 'for the time being' (which could mean indefinitely). Wonder if it would work with maths? Probably not, even grown-ups can't be that thick (well, not all of them).

Saturday 9th

Went with family to see Grandad. The journey was so long I told Dad I was going to be sick, thus forcing him to stop the car at the next motorway services. Lost Dad £5 on the fruit machines there.

When we finally arrived Grandad gave me £5 which I pocketed quickly, dead scared Dad would claim it for the money I'd lost on the fruit machines.

Sunday 10th
Stayed in bed.

Monday 11th

I brought up the topic of my birthday present today with my Mum and said that a nice bike (BMX?) would be the best thing because it would save her my bus fare to school and make me more independent. She must have got the message because later on that day when we went out shopping, I saw her looking at prices in a cycle magazine in the newsagents.

Tuesday 12th

This morning I decided my parents weren't giving me enough to eat. So I told Mum I had a friend coming round for dinner and that she had an enormous appetite. Mum agreed to buy lots of extra food when she went shopping to compensate for my friend's visit. Later on, when Mum came back, her bags were absolutely packed full of all my favourite foods.

Sadly, after Mum had prepared the meal, I had to tell her that my friend's father had phoned to say that my friend had had an accident and wouldn't be able to come for dinner. Mum looked dismayed, saying 'Oh no, what on earth shall I do with all this food?' I comforted her by saying that as she had bought it all because of me, it was down to me to dispose of it.

Wednesday 13th

Gran (Mum's Mum) came to stay for an indefinite period. Terrible. She complained to Dad and Mum that they were bringing me up wrongly: 'That child gets away with murder. He's lazy and treats you like servants. He should be made to do some of the work around the house.' Considered putting superglue in her false teeth cleaner to shut her up, but dismissed this as too obvious, I'd be bound to get caught.

Dad and Mum, terrified of her, made me wash up. Immediate 'accident': broke the coronation mug that Gran gave Mum. This got me out of the rest of the washing-up, but Gran insisted I was sent to bed without any supper. This is going to be a tough time. If I hadn't had the foresight to lay in a supply of food from the fridge, I'd be in trouble.

Thursday 14th

More pressure on me (as a result of Gran) to help about the house: wash up, dust, vacuum, clean windows, etc. My standard excuses to get out of such chores (growing pains throughout body; allergy to dust; fear of electrocution by household appliances; breakages, etc.) met a complete stone wall.

Finally I was forced to clean the outsides of the windows. (Shall look up the number of the NSPCC later.) It was the humiliation I couldn't stand, especially when I was spotted by that idiot Mark Thomson from my class. I had to pretend to him it was all part of a ruse, but I was so put out I accidentally broke a window. Any other time this would have been a good dodge, but not so soon after the coronation mug, and not with Gran around.

The end result (suggested by Gran, of course) is that I lose my pocket money until the broken window is paid for. That woman has got to go!

Friday 15th

Decided to use totally different strategy: Operation Be-Nice-To-Grandma. Took Grandma early morning cup of tea in bed. Mum and Dad think I'm wonderful, Gran impressed as well. Gran kept in bathroom for hours by laxative I'd put in her tea. Dad annoyed, unable to get into bathroom. Gran insisted it was 'something she ate' – Mum upset by this slur on her cooking.

I suggested that Mum and Dad call in the doctor to look at Gran. Gran touched by my concern for her.

Saturday 16th

Early morning tea for Gran again (no laxative this time, otherwise she'd get suspicious). While she drank I asked after her health and received a complete list of ailments from migraine in the head to bunions on the feet. That's where all the Health Service money goes! I told her she could count on me to help her. She, touched, said she wished other people in our house showed as much concern.

In an effort to be 'helpful', I thought it a good idea to pass this on to Dad and Mum. Dad rather put out at suggestion that he shows no concern for Gran. Mum says Gran has a point.

Dad not talking to Mum. Mum, still miffed over yesterday's dig at her cooking, not talking to Gran. Their not talking to one another is very useful, as they can't double-check the hints I drop about what each has been saying about the other.

Sunday 17th

Remove colour supplements from Sunday papers as soon as they are delivered, and leave them in Gran's room. Deny all knowledge when asked if I've seen them.

Mum finds them four hours later. Gran claims Dad must have left them there, 'He's always been one for leaving things lying around.'

Decided now was a good time to increase pressure: added extra salt to Mum's Sunday dinner. Dad silent on subject (from bitter experience). Gran complained volubly. Mum peeved at Gran.

Monday 18th

Stuck hairs from Dad's shaving brush on bar of Gran's special soap in bathroom. Furious row.

Atmosphere too hostile for anyone to notice me, except to use me as confidant to complain about the others. (Gone are the days of ordering me to wash up.)

Gran sees me as her only friend in this house, tells me she plans to cut Dad and Mum out of her will and leave everything to me. I murmur 'No you shouldn't', but wonder how I can find out how much she's got?

Tuesday 19th

Boy next door called in for few minutes. I blamed him for the whoopee cushion on Gran's chair. (As expected, due to tension between them, Dad fell about as Gran sat on whoopee cushion.) Gran furious.
Gran left.

Later admitted to Dad and Mum separately that I was the culprit. As expected, they were both grateful. Both complimented me on my honesty, and both gave me a pound.

Wednesday 20th
Discussion at school on future careers. Perky Parrott said with my talents I was ideally suited to politics. From what I've heard about politicians, he could be right.

The end